Barack Obama

Other Books by Libby Hughes

Bali
Margaret Thatcher
Benazir Bhutto
Norman Schwarzkopf
Colin Powell
Valley Forge
West Point
Nelson Mandela
Yitzhak Rabin
Christopher Reeve
Tiger Woods
George W. Bush
John Grisham
Ronald Reagan
American Genius: Henry Wadsworth Longfellow

Barack Obama

✦

Voice of Unity, Hope, and Change

Libby Hughes

iUniverse, Inc.

New York Bloomington Shanghai

Barack Obama
Voice of Unity, Hope, and Change

Copyright © 2008 by Libby Hughes

iUniverse books may be ordered through booksellers or by contacting:

iUniverse
1663 Liberty Drive
Bloomington, IN 47403
www.iuniverse.com
1-800-Authors (1-800-288-4677)

Because of the dynamic nature of the Internet, any Web addresses or links contained in this book may have changed since publication and may no longer be valid.

The views expressed in this work are solely those of the author and do not necessarily reflect the views of the publisher, and the publisher hereby disclaims any responsibility for them.

Photo Credits: Courtesy of Creative Commons; www.barackobama.com; Google free photos

ISBN: 978-0-595-51404-5 (pbk)
ISBN: 978-0-595-61885-9 (ebk)

Printed in the United States of America

For Rebecca, who is fearless and full of hope.

Contents

Introduction

The life story, so far, of Barack Obama is extraordinary, and he is a great role model for young adults. His gifts for speechmaking, as well as his winning smile and handsome appearance, are all bonuses to a promising, national political career in a possible international arena.

His multi-racial heritage between a white mother from Kansas and a black father from Kenya bring the merging of two continents onto the American stage of politics in a unique way.

Obama's birth in Hawaii and early years in Indonesia were of special interest to this writer, who also lived in Indonesia just after the coup of Sukarno, Indonesia's leader for several decades. A book on Bali resulted. Furthermore, this writer lived in a thatched cottage on a coffee and tea farm in the Highlands outside Nairobi, Kenya, while she was acting with a professional British Company at the Kenya National Theatre, and her husband was covering the Mau Mau rebellion.

From there, she and her former husband drove from Nairobi to the border of Sudan and then 6,000 miles south to Cape Town, South Africa, in a Volkswagen bug with a Labrador Retriever. Many stops found them under a classic baobab tree, eating a can of tuna fish and a can of peas while savoring the incredible scenes of Africa with the belly of a round sun, silhouetting the claws of the baobab tree. Sometimes there was only a dirt road for a highway or a narrow strip of tarmac for the Volkswagen bug to set one front tire and one back tire. In the wilderness, there would be only a round thatched hut for a hotel. African chiefs in villages along the way would offer her a sack of potatoes or a fat pig as a sign of friendship and hospitality. Even a full-grown Cheetah was offered as a gift. She would have to make a delicate refusal and drive to the next destination.

For six years, Hughes lived in Africa, based out of Cape Town, South Africa, and another six years in Asia, based in Hong Kong.

The dramatic beauty of Hawaii; the raw beauty in Africa; and the incredible beauty of Asia with its centuries of history make for an original backdrop to writing about a 2008 presidential candidate.

With this commonality in certain locations in Obama's life, this writer found his biographical highlights intriguing. Also, Obama's identity crisis as a teenager and young man is something that young adults can relate to in their own lives.

Libby Hughes, Cambridge, Massachusetts, 2008

1

Romance in Hawaii

Say the word "Hawaii."

It is a melodic and romantic name for America's 50th state. Images of wrinkled mountains with lush trees in a dark green jade, cascading down the slopes to the beaches below, licked by white caps from teal-green waters, are images that rise in thought. We imagine islands that are festooned with orchids, birds of paradise, ginger blossoms, and necklaces of flowers placed around the necks of visitors to welcome them with ALOHA! This is the Hawaii both in reality and in our mind's eye.

The string of islands or Hawaii's archipelago numbers nineteen islands, including atolls and islets. Volcanoes make up the watery underbelly of the whole string. Because of its geological formation, Hawaii is vulnerable to earthquakes and tsunamis as well as gradual erosion over time.

For Barack Obama, Hawaii would become his birthplace on August 4, 1961 and his home during early parts of his life. He would absorb the beauty, color, and surf that are unique to Hawaii.

Say the word "Honolulu."

The city itself has a mystical name, meaning a city sheltered from the wind. Yet, it is like many tropical cities with palm trees and souvenir shops, lining major streets and boulevards. The brightly colored Moo Moos, which are large roomy caftans for women, blow from their hangers in ocean breezes and are the most popular souvenirs aside from surfboards and necklaces. Electronic shops and western music throb and beat in between the enchantment of Hawaii. Here, East meets West in culture and the arts.

Say the name "O'ahu."

This is the largest of the Hawaiian Islands—600 square miles with 112 miles of beaches in a sandy necklace around the whole island. Waikiki Beach is the most popular among tourists. The waves on this southeast coast are gentle as compared to the big crashing waves on the North Shore. From Waikiki Beach, the Diamond Head Volcano is in full view. The 760 foot, volcano is extinct, but its cone shape is an exotic backdrop to Waikiki Beach, not far from the Honolulu capitol.

Under these idyllic conditions, two young people met and fell in love. They came from two different continents. The white girl, Stanley Ann Dunham, was from the North American continent and the African boy, Barack Obama, from the continent of Africa. Their student days at the University of Hawaii brought them together in a Russian class. They became mother and father to America's Barack Obama.

Before detailing the romance, let's dip into the background of each parent.

First, there was Barack's mother and her parents. She was Stanley Ann Dunham. Stanley? A boy's name for a girl? Why? Her father, Stanley Dunham, wanted a boy, so he tacked his own first name onto the birth certificate of his daughter.

Kansas is right in the middle of the United States. A dome of blue sky seems to fit right over the whole state with clouds practically kissing the rolling hills and swaying cornstalks. Wichita, Kansas, was the place where Barack's grandparents met and where his mother was born.

Stanley Dunham (Barack's grandfather) was a wild young man. He could be compared to the character of Fonzi, the actor Henry Winkler played in a television series called "Happy Days." Winkler had black hair, slicked back just like Stanley's. Mischievous and uncontrollable in high school in Wichita, Kansas, Stanley was suspended after punching the school principal in the nose at the age of fifteen and fled Kansas for Chicago and California. Like a hobo, Stanley jumped onto cattle cars and storage cars of trains and made his way north and west. However, he always came back to Kansas.

On one of these return trips, Stanley met a pretty girl, Madelyn, of English and Scots descent (and possibly Cherokee, too). Soon they were dating, although Madelyn's parents were not happy with this wild and blustery young man. Love won out and they eloped. With World War II on the horizon, Stanley Dunham joined the army. Madelyn had to work in a factory near his base, while taking care of her baby in between shifts.

Upon Stanley's return from the service overseas, the couple and their daughter were constantly moving. First, they went to Berkeley, California, for Stanley to attend the University of California with the aid of the G.I. Bill. Stanley quickly tired of academics, and they returned to Kansas where Stanley worked in a furniture store. Next, they went to a small town in Texas for a job in another store. The Dunhams had no racial prejudice and when their small daughter, Stanley Ann, befriended a black girl, they were attacked and reprimanded by neighbors.

That episode drove the Dunhams far away to Seattle, Washington, where they stayed for young Ann Dunham to finish high school. The furniture store transferred Stanley and his family to Honolulu to a branch store. The Dunhams bought a home and began a happy life in Hawaii. Ann Dunham began her freshman year of college at the University of Hawaii in 1959.

While Ann Dunham was growing up in various American states, an African boy, Barack Obama, was growing up in a thatched hut in the East African country of Kenya, near the shores of Lake Victoria. He was a member of the very smart Luo tribe. Young, barefooted Barack was happy herding his father's goats around the dusty village. His father became a cook for members of the British community. Knowing the importance of English, his father sent him to an English-speaking school in a tin roof shack. Little Barack was a bright student. He then was transferred to a private British school in the capital city of Nairobi.

The intellect of Barack Obama senior was so extraordinary that when Kenya achieved its independence from Great Britain, the government established academic relations with some American universities to train and educate their young people so that they could bring education and ideas back to Kenya. That's how 23-year-old Barack Obama was selected to attend the University of Hawaii for study in economics.

There we pick up the story of how Ann Dunham and Barack Obama met at the University of Hawaii at Manoa. Beyond the traffic and tourist haunts of Honolulu, is the peaceful valley of

Manoa with its modern buildings at the university. In a classroom of Russian language, Barack was attracted to the 18-year-old Ann Dunham. They talked about international affairs and the unspeakable racial prejudice in the United States. Ann liked the lanky student's British accent and easy smile. Soon, Ann invited the young man home to dinner to meet her parents. It was not apparent to them that the two young people were falling in love, but they were.

Ann Dunham wondered what the land of Kenya was like. She never visited the land of her husband-to-be, although she was curious, and he described for her the country he loved.

Kenya sits on the Equator in East Africa. It is a country of great beauty and variety. There are mountains, lakes, valleys, and desert as well as a coastline of white beaches, looking across the shimmering waters of the Indian Ocean. Ann could only dream in her mind's eye about Barack Obama's homeland.

The Arab traders plowed through the blue-green Indian Ocean in their dhows, which were sailing vessels with full-blown triangular sails that carried their spices from India and the Arabian peninsulas to the coastal towns of east Africa. They also brought Islam to African shores.

Between the 15th and 17th centuries, the Luo tribe (Barack's tribe) migrated from southern Sudan to settle on Lake Victoria where African Barack Obama began his young life in the village of Alego. Members of the Luo tribe were considered highly intelligent.

In 1894, Kenya became a British Protectorate and finally a British colony in 1920. Not until 1963 did independence come to Kenya.

Wildlife abounds in Kenya and composes much of the tourist industry, bringing thousands to its land. There is the Tsavo National Park where lions and cheetahs run free. The Amboseli National Park sits near the skirts of the majestic Mt. Kilimanjaro and has a variety of wild animals, including unpredictable rhinos and rogue elephants. Many poachers used to steal into the park and kill elephants for their ivory tusks. A worldwide uproar has helped to stop the hunters.

Masai warriors still live on the flanks of the National Park. They wear deerskin togas and colorful beads in their ears, on their arms, and wrapped around their necks. They still carry spears and drink blood and milk from their cows. The Masai men are famous for surrounding a lion in a circle and capturing it with their spears.

In the park forests are free-running leopards and elephants, viewed from treetop lodges. Lake Naivasha and Lake Nakuru are on the plains and delight the eye from hills above. In the desert, nomadic tribes live.

Nairobi became the capital of Kenya in 1899. At one time, the city was a swamp. The name means "a place of cold water." A modern city of hotels and theatres, Nairobi is a headquarters for tourism. Coffee and tea farms abound in the Highland hills above Nairobi.

Danish author Karen Blixen (Isak Dinesen) lived there in the Ngong Hills and wrote the famed novel, "Out of Africa," which was made into a memorable film.

Ann fell in love with a distant country that she would never see, except through the eyes of Barack senior and their son.

What would these two young people do with their lives?

2

Boyhood in Hawaii and Indonesia

The girl from Kansas and the boy from Kenya married in 1960 and moved into the Dunham household while they continued college at the University of Hawaii. A mixed marriage in those days would have been impossible in the southern states of the mainland, but for Hawaii, it was a natural integration of people from all continents.

The new husband intensified his studies at Hawaii's University, focusing on economics. He seemed to be a natural leader among the students and was elected president of the International Students Association. Ann Dunham Obama also kept studying anthropology at the University.

On August 4, 1961, Ann and Barack added a third member to their little family unit—a baby boy that they named Barack Hussein (after his grandfather) Obama, whom they nicknamed "Barry." The new grandparents, Madelyn and Stanley, were delighted. However, four adults and one baby meant higher costs. The wages in the furniture store were not enough to support them all. Madelyn Dunham found a job in a bank as a secretary to extend the family finances.

In 1963, the handsome Kenyan graduated first in his class academically. The prestigious Harvard University in Cambridge, Massachusetts, gave him a full scholarship. The whole family was proud and excited, but Ann could not go with her husband because the funds didn't cover a wife and son. The separation was painful for Ann and a loss for her son.

At the end of his time at Harvard, Barack Obama decided to return to Kenya without Ann and Barry. He had a wife and children in his home country. The Luo tribe allowed its men to have more than one wife. It was an accepted part of their culture.

The long absence from his family in Hawaii and his obligation to his Kenyan family resulted in a divorce from Ann and separation from his two-year-old son. Barack also had a responsibility to his country to return and use his education and expertise to help Kenya and its people prosper. This was a sad reality for his ex-wife in Hawaii.

Barry missed having a father in his life even though his mother and grandparents were attentive and loving. To Barry, Stanley became known as Gramps and Madelyn became "Tutu" (Hawaiian for grandmother) or "Toot" as she was called affectionately by Barry.

Gramps tried to do many things with Barry that his father might have done. The old man and boy went spear-fishing at Kailua Bay or they would watch the astronauts from the Apollo Mission land at Hickam Air Force Base. Barry always remembered that exciting event.

Because Stanley had an outgoing personality, he made many friends of all races through the furniture business. He joked with them and established special friendships. Barry went to markets with Gramps or watched him play checkers in the local park. Toot was working all day at the bank.

By the time Barry was four-years-old, another man came into his mother's life. Ann was an attractive young woman with a heart-shaped face and long brown hair. Lolo Soetoro was a University of Hawaii student of geology from Indonesia. Like most Indonesians, Lolo was well-mannered, soft-spoken, and filled with sweetness. Gramps enjoyed playing endless games of chess with him, and Barry arm-wrestled with him. He was a happy male addition to the household.

When Barry turned six-years-old, Lolo had finished his studies and was planning to return to Indonesia. He proposed to Barry's mother, who accepted his offer of marriage. Lolo flew back first to make preparations for the arrival of his bride and step-son. Gramps and Toot were uneasy about their daughter and grandson going to such a distant country. The capital city of Jakarta was embroiled in political unrest, which caused them concern. Nevertheless, they supported their daughter in her choices.

Indonesia, like Hawaii, has a string of islands, numbering 17,500 in its archipelago in Southeast Asia. The country has a mystique and enchantment for tourists as well as residents. It is rich in oil, spices, and the cotton fabric called batik, made from vegetable dyes.

In the 13th century, spice traders from Southeast Asia brought trade and the Islam religion to the shores of Indonesia as they had done in East Africa; especially Kenya. The Dutch ruled Indonesia for more than three centuries until the Japanese occupied the country during World War II. Once the war was over in 1945, Sukarno became Indonesia's first president.

Most of the more than 222 million people are Muslims although Buddhists, Hindus, Christians, and animists compose the minority religions.

When the day came for Ann and Barry to arrive at Jakarta's airport in 1967, Lolo was there to meet them. The steamy heat was almost suffocating, but they were all happy to see each other. Lolo rented a car to take them to their new home outside the city limits of Jakarta. They crossed a small wooden bridge over a river to get to the compound.

During the ride to his new home, Barry was looking at all the sights from the back window. He saw people wearing wide-brimmed straw hats as they bent over the flooded rice paddies, pulling green shoots. Boys straddled water buffaloes, harnessed to crude wooden plows, sloshing through rows of green rice blades, poking through the water.

The open air stucco house, covered by red tiles, was surrounded by animals that Lolo had collected. From New Guinea, Lolo brought Barry a small gibbon tied down by a chain. There were chickens and a dog—everything a young boy could want. The house had no indoor plumbing. Relief from the oppressive heat of the day came from large umbrella trees, providing shade. At night they all slept under mosquito nets. The night air spread a sweet fragrance from the frangipani trees and bushes, not unlike the smell of honeysuckle in America. Barry thought that this new country and his home were exciting.

Lolo turned out to be a caring step-father. When a neighboring boy threw a rock at Barry's head, Lolo thought it was the time to teach Barry the art of self-defense. The next day, he brought home two pairs of boxing gloves and spent hours in the yard, teaching Barry how to protect himself and how to go on the attack.

There were also things Barry thought he could only discuss with a man and not his mother, such as the strength of a man. Barry saw his mother give money to any beggar on the street or to anyone who came to the door, asking for money. Lolo taught him the wisdom of not giving away everything he had and advised him about saving his money.

To add to the family's income, Ann started work right away at the American Embassy in Jakarta, teaching English to Indonesian businessmen. Because Lolo and Ann didn't make enough money to send Barry to a private school, Barry first attended a Catholic School and then a Muslim Public School where students were the sons of farmers and servants, rather than the children of diplomats. Whatever the religious teachings, his mother was more interested in the academics. She felt they were not up to American standards and she sent away for academic materials. To keep him stimulated, Ann woke Barry up at four in the morning to learn through the use of flash cards. Barry wasn't thrilled about it and longed to sleep two more hours, but he followed his mother's directive and yawned through most of these sessions.

More important than academics, Barry's mother wanted him to become a fine human being. She instilled in him her own sense of moral values. Although she was not affiliated with any particular church, she told him that honesty and fairness along with exercising good judgment were essential to building character in life.

From young Barry's viewpoint, life in Indonesia was a great adventure from eating strange foods to playing games with his school friends. However, Barry began to notice that Lolo and his mother did not relate or talk to each other very much as they had done in Hawaii. They had been apart one year after Lolo was called back by his government and was sent to New Guinea. Now that they were together, things were strained between them. In fact, Lolo was more attentive to Barry than to his wife.

The 1960s were a stormy time in Indonesia. Politically, there was unrest. Students were protesting against the government, and the influence of communism was growing. The military and Indonesian people were unhappy with Sukarno's dictatorship and his flirtations with the communists. On September 30, 1965, a violent overthrow of Sukarno began, and soon thereafter, Indonesia became ruled by General Suharto.

In this climate of uncertainty, Barry's mother became increasingly concerned for her son's welfare. What would she decide about Barry's future?

3

Back to Hawaii

It took a whole year for Barry's mother to decide what was best for Barry. Within that year, a new sister, Maya, arrived and made a special addition to the Soetoros.

Meanwhile, daily life became a little better for Lolo and his family. Through a relative, he found a job in an American oil company, which moved them to a better home and standard of living. However, bribery, dishonesty, and corruption were a frustrating aspect of life within the country that troubled Barry's mother.

Her role model for her son continued to be Barry's biological father from Kenya. She reminded Barry that poverty did not stop him from progressing in life. Through honesty and superior intelligence, his father had moved from a remote village in East Africa to the famous halls of Harvard University.

Along with his African father, Barry's mother would show her son other black men of honor such as Martin Luther King, Jr., Supreme Court Justice Thurgood Marshall, and actor Sydney Poitier as excellent role models.

After a year, Ann Obama Soetoro made a decision about Barry's future schooling. Ann had exhausted all her educational tools for teaching Barry and told him it was best for him to return to Hawaii to live with his grandparents. There, he would go to Punahou, a private school in Honolulu.

In 1971 Barry was sent alone on an airplane from Jakarta to Honolulu. The very excited Gramps and Toot were there to meet him. Since Barry had last seen them, they had sold their house and moved into a two bedroom apartment near the school. Gramps was now selling insurance, and Toot had worked her way up to vice-president of her bank. Gramps was not as successful at selling insurance as he had been with furniture. But he still had dreams of writing poetry and designing his dream home.

The Punahou School, which means "spring of clear water," was founded in 1841 by Congregational missionaries. The 76 acres stretch along the Manoa Valley with its exotic white and yellow blossoms dotted across the campus. It still remains the largest independent school in the United States. The architecture is a mixture of traditional and modern.

Gramps thought the school environment was heaven. He proudly accompanied Barry to his first day in fifth grade. They were early and sat next to a Chinese boy, who was also new. Barry and the boy jabbered to each other while Gramps made jokes, putting them both at ease.

Once inside his homeroom, the teacher took roll call and announced Barry's name as "Barack Obama." His classmates laughed at the strange sounding name and made him feel embarrassed. However, his homeroom teacher, Mrs. Hefty, immediately put him at ease by saying it was a beautiful name. Because she had lived in Kenya, teaching school, she was familiar with the country and names of the people. She also wanted to know to which tribe his father belonged. When Barry replied "Luo," his class again broke into laughter.

The focus on his name and tribe caused Barry to be the object of teasing. The boys called him a "monkey." It was cruel and hurtful. Young Barry withdrew into his own lonely world. Instead of playing football or soccer after school, he went directly home to do his homework and go with Gramps to pick up Toot from the bank.

However, Barry invented a story about his father, which he told his friends in school. He proudly announced that his father was an African chief. Underneath his confident exterior was a very insecure ten-year-old boy.

Before Christmas, Toot suddenly announced that Barry's father would be coming to spend Christmas with them and stay a month to see his son. Barry's mother would also come from Indonesia to see them. Since their apartment was too small, Gramps and Toot found a small apartment to rent for their visitors.

With this news, Barry was afraid. This would be his first meeting with his real father and he was uncertain how it would be.

Since his father's divorce from his mother, he had remarried and had five sons and one daughter. The purpose of Barack Obama's trip to Hawaii was to see his son, but also to recover from a car accident that left him with a limp.

Their first time meeting took place at the apartment, and it was awkward. To Barry, his father seemed very tall and thin behind thick glasses. The absent father reached into his bag and pulled out some typical woodcarvings from Kenya of an elephant, lion, and a man in tribal costume. Barry thanked him for the presents, but the man was still a stranger to him.

One day during his father's visit, Barry's teacher Mrs. Hefty called his grandmother to ask if Barry's father could speak to his class. Toot accepted for her ex-son-in-law. When the day arrived, Barry was very apprehensive and embarrassed about his father's presence in his classroom, but it turned out to be a big success. His Kenyan father told about the wildlife and tribes in Kenya and about the country's independence from Great Britain. His teacher and classmates were impressed, and Barry became a hero.

On Christmas day, Barry received a basketball from his father. The only photographs of father and son were taken that day. Some of Barry's memories of his father were of the two of them reading books together or watching his father sway to the music of Africa or the sound of his father's laughter.

And then, he was gone—gone back to Kenya—gone from his life.

How would this affect his adolescent years?

4

Troubled Years

Barry gave the impression of being a happy boy to his friends and teachers during his seven years at Punahou School.

As he grew taller, his interest in basketball grew, too. The basketball his father had given him was a prized possession. He was always shooting baskets through school hoops both inside and outside. His coach called him a "gym rat."

Coach McLachlin grinned at the recollection of young Barack Obama. "He loved the game so much that he'd do anything to practice. He snuck past teachers when they opened the gym's locked doors. When no one was around, he broke into the gym."

During his junior and senior years in high school, Barack found himself on the basketball team as a six foot two inch forward. The team placed second in state playoffs when he was a junior and first when a senior.

In honor of his hero, Michael Jordan, Barack wore a number 23 jersey. Because Barack was left-handed, his coach pitted him against left-handed players on opposing teams.

Soon after Barack's father returned to Kenya from his visit to his son, Ann's relationship to Lolo fell apart, and she came back to Hawaii with Maya, Barack's half sister. The three moved into their own apartment while Ann entered graduate school at the

University of Hawaii to earn her masters degree in anthropology. This put added stress upon the family finances. Barack had to find odd jobs suitable for a teenager. Dishing up ice cream, babysitting Maya, and buying food were some of the responsibilities he had to assume.

Sometimes, without Toot's knowledge, Gramps would take Barack at the age of twelve to dark lit nightclubs. The two would sit at the bar as Barry sipped a Coke and watched billiard games or listened to jukebox music. Gramps was discouraged over his failure as an insurance salesman. These night visits relaxed him.

Field research was required for his mother's degree, which meant she had to return to Indonesia for that research. Obviously Maya would have to go with her, and Ann wanted Barack to go with them. But Barack wanted to stay at Punahou and in Hawaii.

Was that the real reason or was there something else that influenced his decision?

Because Barack was the only African/American in his school of Caucasians and Asians, he had a hard time fitting into the social scene. When Ray, another African/American, arrived from Los Angeles, Barack was glad to have someone with whom he could hang out.

Girls were another unknown for Barack. His friend Ray asked white girls out for a date, but they rejected him. Though Barack wouldn't admit it to Ray, he was too shy to ask a girl for a date. Discrimination even reached to the football field for Ray and sometimes to the basketball court for Barack.

In the relationship with Ray, Barack was the moderator and voice of reason in all their discussions. Even then, he reasoned like a lawyer—a lawyer that he would become in the future.

Those teenage years for Barack were like any boy of any race. It was a time of moodiness, pimples, girl curiosity, learning to drive, and asserting independence.

He had three years of living alone with his mother and Maya. Although he had all the symptoms of a teenager, who was trying to transition from boy to young man, Barack's ties to his mother remained strong—even when she went back to Indonesia. He resumed life with Gramps and Toot, who gave him free rein as long as he wasn't a problem.

The biggest challenge for Barack was finding out who he was, and how he fit into a white world. These inner feelings tormented him. He sought comfort in music, dancing, and sports. They eased his mental pain. On the basketball court, he felt the excitement and companionship of his teammates. For a few hours, he forgot his troubles because color didn't matter in the game—winning did.

However, in his lonely moments, the racial slights still hurt. Barack stacked them up in a file in his mind. He remembered being called "coon" or a teacher telling him that his color would rub off if he touched anything or the white peoples' fear of a young black man going to rob them or stalk them.

From Ray's example, Barack started bad-mouthing "white folks." He criticized them until he remembered that his mother and grandparents were white. He felt torn in half. But being black in Hawaii was better than being black in the American south. For a number of years, it was terrifying for Barack to be a man of color in a white man's world.

To sort out his identity, Barack found books in the library, written by black authors, to see how they felt; how they wrestled with discrimination; and how they rose above it. The Black Muslim Malcolm X's (who inspired the teachings of the Black Panthers) autobiography seemed to answer some of his questions. Barack admired Malcolm's demand for respect and his willingness to live alongside his white brothers.

Just as Barack was coming to terms with his bi-racial heritage, there was an incident with his grandparents that set him back. Toot had been harassed for money by a poor man at the bus stop. She was so upset that she wanted Gramps to drive her to work. They argued. Barack tried to play peacemaker, but when Gramps told him the man was black, he felt devastated. Once again the color of his skin thrust him into despair.

Not knowing how to deal with his own despondency, Barack went to an 80-year-old friend of Gramps, who was black. He lived in a poor section near Waikiki beach. Barack told the old man about the incident, Apparently, the man had come from Kansas and knew Gramps and Toot in their young days. He said that the grandparents would never know the real life and feelings of blacks. He explained why blacks developed such hate towards the world of whites. "You might as well get used to it," he said.

Barack left the man feeling depressed. "I felt utterly alone" were the words in his autobiography, *Dreams from My Father.*

With nowhere to turn, Barack turned to alcohol and drugs, so he could erase those questions about race, which troubled him. In his senior year, Barack's mother returned to Hawaii. She put pressure on Barack to apply himself at school and get his grades up for college. Because of her badgering, he pulled himself together, graduated from Punahou, and was accepted at a few good colleges. He chose Occidental College in Los Angeles because he knew of a certain girl going there.

Oxy (the nickname) reminded him of Hawaii. Near Pasadena, the rich colors of flowers, endless days of sunshine, and the stucco buildings with red tile roofs reminded him of home. There were more blacks on campus than at Punahou, but the discussions about race were the same. Barack still felt like a half-breed.

During his Freshman and Sophomore years, Barack involved himself in current affairs, especially about South Africa. He favored putting economic sanctions on the country to stop apartheid. When Barack gave a speech, people really listened to him. He began feeling better about himself.

His appreciation for a first class education made him reconsider Occidental. He wanted to change. Where would he go?

5

Columbia University

New York City would be far different from 365 days of sunshine in California. Although Barack would also miss the sunkissed days of Hawaii, his mind was focused on serious studying.

Once he had learned of a transfer and exchange program between Occidental and Columbia University in New York City, he applied. Oxy had been great, but not challenging enough to stretch Barack's thirst for knowledge. Naturally, leaving good friends behind was the difficult part.

Columbia University had a tradition and history, which appealed to Barack. In 1754 it was known as King's College, named after King George II of England, and considered the fifth oldest college in the United States. The first Trinity Church Schoolhouse was located in lower Manhattan. The Reverend Dr. Samuel Johnson, an American educator and philanthropist, taught there and became president. In 1784 the name of the college changed to Columbia University. By 1867, the college moved to 49th Street and Madison Avenue.

Because the school kept expanding, Columbia's president, Seth Lowe, moved the entire campus to Morningside Heights at 116th Street and Broadway on the City's Upper West Side in 1897. Here, there were three undergraduate schools and thirteen graduate schools. Washington Heights became the second campus for all the Medical Schools.

The architecture in Morningside Heights was designed in the Roman, neo-classical style. Many distinguished graduates passed through Columbia's curriculum: such as John Jay (America's first Secretary of the Treasury).

Barack Obama's majors would be Political Science and International Relations.

His arrival in the summer of 1981 gave him time to settle into special living arrangements. Before leaving Oxy, he had sent deposit money for an apartment in Spanish Harlem near the campus. When he arrived late one night from the West Coast, the apartment was locked and vacant. He did not have enough money to pay for a hotel.

Dejected, Barack hauled all his belongings to the front steps of the apartment house and sat for a long time, pondering his next move. His thoughts wandered to his father, living in Kenya and very far removed from young Barack's daily life. He thought about his black friends at Oxy who had graduated and were moving in their own career paths. His thoughts narrowed to Marcus, his good friend who couldn't seem to find his identity and place in society.

Such rambling thoughts didn't bring him closer to a place to sleep. In desperation, he gathered his luggage and headed for an alley where he would spend his first night in New York City, Briefly, he led the life of a homeless soul.

In the morning, Barack called a Pakistani man he knew on the Upper East Side of Manhattan. Sadik welcomed him into his apartment and listened to the young college student unveil his inner most feelings about life and making a difference in the world. Sadik laughed at him and explained how New Yorkers were only interested in themselves and no one else. Finally, Barack was able to get into the apartment on 109th Street. When that lease expired, Sadik and Barack shared an apartment near East Harlem.

New York City seemed like a foreign land to young Barack, and he covered every inch of it on foot or by running three miles each day. Sadik tried to coax him into a social life, but Barack was committed to his homework. Like Gramps, he tried to put his feelings into poetry and kept a journal of his impressions.

The sounds of New York fascinated him as did the rich neighborhoods and poor neighborhoods.

Here is a sample of some of his thoughts:

"It was as if all middle ground had collapsed, utterly. And nowhere, it seemed, was that collapse more apparent than in the black community I had so lovingly imagined and within which I had hoped to find refuge. I might meet a black friend at his Midtown law firm and before heading to lunch at MoMA (Modern Museum of Art), I would look out across the city toward the East River from his high-rise office, imagining a satisfactory life for myself—a vocation, a family, a home. Until I noticed that the only other blacks in the office were messengers or clerks, the only blacks in the museum were blue-jacketed security guards who counted the hours before they could catch their train home to Brooklyn or Queens," he wrote in his autobiography.

In later years, his thoughts matured and he took a more objective view of life.

"Life appears to be hard sometimes, because life *is* hard sometimes. None of us have control of the circumstances into which we are born. We may be born into poverty or in a country torn by war. For African-Americans, we have additional hurdles to overcome—the legacy of slavery and Jim Crow, and the ongoing problems of discrimination.

Despite all that, our life is what we make it. Those who achieve don't waste time on self-pity or on how unfair life is, nor do they blame others for their problems. Instead, they strive for excellence and take responsibility for their actions, focusing not just on themselves, but on others."

In the summer of 1982, Barack found a construction job to pay his bills. During the summer, his mother and sister Maya came from Hawaii to New York to visit him. They went sightseeing during the day and told Barack of their adventures over dinner. His mother was satisfied by Barack's intense focus on his studies, and they reminisced over stories of the past about her husband, Barack's father, and marveled at his brilliant mind. Barack still felt troubled by his father's infrequent contacts with him over a period of ten years. His mother's stories brought him to life once again.

"She saw my father as everyone hopes at least one other person might see him; she had tried to help the child who never knew him see him in the same way," Barack wrote in his autobiography.

His mother also shared the background of her relationship to his father in Hawaii. He learned that Gramps and Tutu were not in favor of the marriage, but they couldn't stop it. Also,

Barack's grandfather in Kenya strongly opposed a marriage to a white woman. Going back to Kenya with a white wife and multi-racial son would have been dangerous at the time. Therefore, they divorced.

Soon after the visit from his mother and sister, Barack received a telephone call from Nairobi, Kenya, with devastating news. His 46-year-old father had been killed in an automobile accident. His heart went cold. All the dreams of a visit to Kenya in 1983 were dashed. He called his mother to tell her the news. She wept uncontrollably over the telephone. It was a chapter that would never end for Barack.

Not until another year passed was young Barack able to shed tears for his deceased father. It came in a dream where Barack was traveling in a bus with people he didn't know. He entered a big hotel lobby and there was a piano. A man sat down and then a little girl. A whole parade of people passed through the lobby. Then, in the dream, Barack was back on the bus. When he stepped out, it was a courtroom where a judge said it was time to release his father from jail. Barack enters a cell and embraces his father, now old and thin. Barack can't stop crying. Barack's father says, "Barack, I always wanted to tell you how much I love you." Barack awoke from the dream still weeping. Even in death, Barack's father still had an influence on him.

As graduation from Columbia approached in 1983, the idealistic Barack Obama wanted to get involved in the civil rights movement that inspired him through his mother's vivid accounts. It wasn't that easy. His resumes were rejected.

The new graduate had to find a job to support himself. He landed a job at the Business International Corporation, which assisted companies abroad. Barack became an editor of a newsletter in its international financial information division. This job paid well. He had his own office and secretary and was paying off his debts. The good life was pulling him away from his ideals of serving others.

But a telephone call changed all that. His half-sister Auma, who was studying in Germany, wanted to come to visit him. Barack was excited and made preparations for her arrival. Before she was to come, there was another call from her. This time his half-brother had been killed in a motorcycle accident in Kenya. Auma did not come. Somehow that tragedy turned his thought back to civil rights. Several months later, Barack resigned from his comfortable job.

Barack disagreed with the Reagan economic policies. "Change won't come from the top, I would say. Change will come from a mobilized grass roots."

The black security guard at his office building was distressed by the young man's decision. "Mr. Barack, I hope you don't mind if I give you a little bit of advice. You don't have to take it, now, but I'm gonna give it to you anyhow. Forget about this organizing business and do something that's gonna make you some money. Not greedy, you understand. But enough. I'm telling you this 'cause I can see potential in you. Young man like you, got a nice voice—hell, you could be one of them announcers on TV. Or sales … got a nephew about your age making some real money there. That's what we need, see.... You can't help folks that ain't gonna make it nohow, and they won't appreciate you trying. Folks that wanna make it, they gonna find a way to do it on they own.... Don't waste your youth, Mr. Barack. Wake up one morning, an old man like me, and all you gonna be is tired, with nothing to show for it."

Finally, after a six-month struggle of being broke and eating practically nothing, Barack received a phone call from Marty Kaufman in Chicago. He offered Barack a job at $10,000 a year to come to the South Side of Chicago to become a community organizer—finding jobs and establishing training centers for blacks. When the two met in New York, both men were skeptical of each other. Marty was white, which raised Barack's suspicions. Marty felt Barack must be an angry young man if he wanted to become a community organizer, but Marty needed a black man to work in the black communities. Barack was the man.

Although everyone thought Barack was crazy, he was happy, and Chicago was the place to fulfill his long-held dream.

What would his life be like?

6

Fighting Chicago's Poverty

Within a week of being hired, Barack was on his way to Chicago, receiving $2,000 from Kaufman for a car.

Marty Kaufman explained how Barack should operate as a community organizer.

"Most of our work is with churches. If poor and working-class people want to build real power, they have to have some sort of institutional base. With the unions in the shape they're in, the churches are the only game in town. That's where the people are, and that's where the values are, even if they've been buried ... Churches won't work with you, though, just out of the goodness of their hearts. They'll talk a good game—a sermon on Sunday, maybe, or a special offering for the homeless. But if push comes to shove, they won't really move unless you can show them how it'll help them pay their heating bill."

Barack arrived in Chicago in July of 1985. The time was perfect for an eager young man. Before starting work, he swung through the tourist attractions and stared across the wide horizon of Lake Michigan, whose shores are beneath high-rise apartment blocks in the heart of the city.

In the Hyde Park area, he stumbled into a barber shop where the conversation was about the newly elected black mayor,

Harold Washington. His election gave African/Americans a sense of pride and a feeling of being first-class citizens.

Marty gave him a tour of the seedier parts of Chicago. He showed him the empty steel plant, leaving all races out of work. Despite working side by side at the factory, there were unwritten lines of segregation.

Kaufman had persuaded twenty churches to form the Calumet Community Religious Conference, which joined forces with the Developing Communities Project for job placement.

To introduce him to these groups, Marty took Barack to a school auditorium, where 2,000 people turned up because they were unemployed. They were relieved to find that Barack was black and not white like Marty. There was entertainment. The governor came and said a few words. Most important, the churches were there.

Barack Obama was a good listener and people told him their personal stories. A big man named Will told him how he had come back from Vietnam and was hired by a bank. His pay check was good and he had hope for the future. Suddenly, he was laid off and faced an uncertain future until he became a janitor in a church.

Marty's first assignment for Barack was to talk to people and find out the major issues they cared about. It wasn't easy. People were suspicious of him. However, once they trusted him, they opened up. Work in the public sector gave blacks better pay and better benefits. They bought houses in the white neighborhoods, and the whites moved out. The neighborhoods declined.

When he turned in his report to Marty, he said, "Not bad." Then, he gave Barack more advice.

"If you want to organize people, you need to steer away from the peripheral stuff and go towards the people's centers. The stuff that makes them tick. Otherwise, you'll never form the relationships you need to get them involved."

Things turned around when Barack befriended Ruby Styles on Chicago's north side. Her teenage son's best friend was shot outside her home. She was worried for the life of her son. Barack arranged for the Baptist Church to host a discussion about gangs. However, one minister dismissed the idea, which killed the discussion.

Discouraged, but not giving up, Barack formed a police meeting and it failed. Marty told him he had to be more specific and not so general when calling groups together. Barack realized that his new job was going to be tough—an uphill battle to win the hearts and minds of his black brothers and sisters.

One of the worst projects in Chicago was on the far south side. It was called Altgeld Gardens. The dirty Calumet River was on one side and a large landfill on the other. The sewage plant was nearby, adding to the strong stench in the project where the poorest of the poor lived. The houses were falling apart and morale was at its lowest. Churches were run by whites and attended by blacks.

Beneath grumbling and complaining from blacks, Barack found some gutsy and humorous black women—single women, raising and supporting families in this horrible ghetto.

Despite their bursts of humor, no one was finding jobs after all the fanfare and promises. The only person they could blame was Marty because he was white.

Finally, the key women behind the scenes wanted to give up. This made Barack angry—angry at himself for ever coming to

Chicago. In his anger, he looked out the window and saw some young black boys playing basketball. This picture of youth gave him ammunition to answer these women and ask them what would happen to young boys on the streets if they gave up.

"You know, I didn't come here 'cause I needed a job. I came here 'cause Marty said there were some people who were serious about doing something to change their neighborhoods. I don't care what's happened in the past. I know that I'm here, and committed to working with you. If there's a problem, then we'll fix it. If you don't think anything's happened after working with me, then I'll be the first to tell you to quit. But if you all are planning to quit now, then I want you to answer my question."

There was dead silence.

Finally, Barack's friend, Will, had an idea. He suggested holding street corner meetings where unemployed people hung out. Back inside the church meetings, Will managed to get people thinking about the GOOD memories at Altgeld and to share them. Pretty soon, everyone had a memory or story to share. Barack began to feel that maybe his job did have meaning after all.

Without big manufacturing plants to solve joblessness, Barack and his small core of organizers tried to find work for people in small shops in nearby Roseland. Barack began reaching out to the city offices for employment and training. He brought them together with the folks from Altgeld, and there was an honest exchange.

Then, Barack experienced his first winter in Chicago. It was a bitter cold that he had not felt in New York City. The wind came off Lake Michigan in a mighty rage, cutting his cheeks and bones like a Siberian winter in Russia. For the young man born in the heat of Hawaii, winter was an adjustment.

Even Marty was concerned about his apprentice because Barack seemed obsessed with his job, leaving no room for a personal life. However, when Barack wasn't working, he was reading books or occasionally socializing with the leaders in Altgeld. He even attended different church services on Sundays. Finally, Barack was getting to know the lives of individuals, and they were confiding in him. He was building trust.

One of his discoveries was the intense hatred against whites and self-hatred of being black. These were forces that were harmful to progress. Furthermore, Barack was troubled by too much talk and not enough action.

◆   ◆   ◆

In the middle of his devotion to his work, Barack's half sister, Auma, arrived in Chicago from Germany to visit him. They talked and talked deep into the night. He opened his heart to her and told her about a white woman in New York, who had captured his heart. But he found that their two worlds were so different. Either he would have to live in hers or she would have to live in his. He broke her heart, but his had been broken, too—not only by her, but by others.

They spoke about their father, the man neither one of them had known very well. According to Auma, their father had come back to Kenya with a white wife, Ruth, whose parents were very rich. Obama senior had a good job with an American Oil Company. His two children from another marriage came to live with them. Ruth and Barack senior soon had two sons of their own. Then, their father went into government, but soon

lost his job. He had no money until he was hired by the government again. He had visited Auma in Germany and was very
kind to her. Auma told her half-brother that their father was
very proud of him. Auma's words seem to fill that empty hole in
his heart and the lost years he never had with his father.

◆   ◆   ◆

When Mayor Washington opened a new employment and
training center in Roseland, Barack began to see the fruits of his
work. At the ceremony, the Mayor charmed everyone. He cut
the ribbon and after fifteen minutes, he was gone in his limousine. So overwhelmed, the lady leader forgot to invite the mayor
to their next rally. Barack threw up his hands in disgust.

Nevertheless, after his first frustrating year in Chicago, there
were small signs of progress—jobs, improved roads, and parks.

But Marty tried to persuade him to go on to other things and
not to waste his youth on Altgeld. What Marty didn't realize
was that Barack had formed personal attachments to these people. He couldn't just leave them.

Not until he met Dr. Martha Collier, the tough principal of
an Altgeld elementary school, did he get over being upset with
Marty. Barack started working with teenage mothers of four-
teen and fifteen years of age and finding out about their young
lives, cut off by early pregnancies. He began working with parents, giving them forms to fill out about the complaints they
had regarding their buildings, apartments, and plumbing.

When there was an issue with possible asbestos in the walls of
Altgeld, Obama's army went downtown to the executive director of Chicago's Housing Authority (CHA) and TV crews
turned up. The Altgeld group had been lied to—no tests had

been taken in their area. Television had shamed the director of CHA to take some kind of action.

A public meeting was arranged with residents of Altgeld. When the director arrived, the TV crews were ready to see him face this hostile audience, not only about asbestos, but regarding broken toilets, mold, and small repairs to run-down homes. However, emotions were running so high that they exploded, and the director escaped to his limousine and sped away. High hopes and high spirits collapsed.

Barack and others began to feel that things were changing; especially among young people. They seemed tougher and hardened. Perhaps drugs were part of it. Preteens had easy access to guns and used them like toys—not aware of the consequences. Although Barack was unafraid, others were afraid.

At least, Barack tried to save the life of one teenager, Ruby's 16-year-old son, who seemed to be drifting into bad habits. Barack invited him to a basketball game where they both played. Kyle's opponent bullied him until Kyle socked him in the jaw. On the way home, Barack lectured the boy and promised not to tell his mother if he stayed out of trouble. The boy promised.

With renewed energy, Barack decided to take on the Chicago school system. He hit a brick wall because many teachers and educators attended the churches he depended on to back him. So, Barack targeted the parents.

Then, he found cooperation with two school officials who worked with him on a youth counseling network. An Illinois state senator promised funding for it. One principal wanted his wife and daughter to work for the program and be on the payroll. Barack was stunned.

After three years, somehow, somewhere, and at some time, Barack Obama decided to apply to several law schools: Yale, Stanford, and Harvard. There was a young man, Johnnie, who had been working alongside him and could take his place. By the time he was ready to leave, the youth program would be well underway. He felt his knowledge of business and law would help him as a community organizer. He tried not to think of law school as an escape from Altgeld and Roseland. And yet, he wanted an affluent life while working to help poor Chicago blacks.

Still working with many churches to join the youth organizations, Barack was uncertain about his own religious feelings until he met Reverend Jeremiah Wright at Trinity's United Church of Christ. The 4,000 members were from working class and there were professionals.

After Mayor Washington died suddenly and Barack was still pushing for school reforms, he received his acceptance from Harvard University. At a meeting with a group of ministers, Barack made his announcement. They were delighted and congratulated him.

For the first time on Sunday morning, Barack put on a suit to attend a service at Trinity Church. The topic of Reverend Wright's sermon was "Audacity of Hope." This title would never be far from his thought in the future.

What would he do before going to Harvard?

7

Kenya: Land of his Father

Before starting Harvard in the fall of 1988, Barack knew it was time to go to Kenya in East Africa. There, at last, he would find relatives and half of his roots, his heritage.

On his way, he stopped in Europe for three weeks to visit the tourist spots. On the European continent, he felt like a misfit—someone who didn't belong—a foreigner.

Barack was eager to get to Kenya. Perhaps he would feel a part of it as if he belonged. There was an excitement as he landed at Kenyatta International Airport outside Nairobi, Kenya. It was dawn and very few people were at the airport. Somehow his bag had not been taken off and was on its way to Johannesburg, South Africa.

A British Airways attendant extended her regrets about his bag. However, she recognized his last name and knew immediately who he was and his family connections. This made him feel good. At that moment, his half-sister Auma appeared and greeted him along with their father's sister Zeitini. Barack and the two women climbed into Auma's blue Volkswagen bug. People were rushing to work on the highway and side dirt roads. It reminded Barack of Indonesia and the early rush to work in a dusty, hazy morning. The car chugged up a hill to a yellow apartment building, next to the university where Auma taught.

Nairobi still had the flavor of British colonialism in its city center although modern high-rises and office buildings dwarfed the colonial architecture. Souvenir shops were everywhere as they were in Hawaii and Indonesia. Barack quickly recognized the small woodcarvings that his father had brought to him as a ten-year-old boy. He felt at home.

In Kenya, there were lingering memories of the Mau Mau rebellion. This was a guerilla operation in the dense bush of Kenya. It was led by Jomo Kenyatta, who tried to attack and scare white farmers to go back to Britain. Eventually, a settlement was made and Kenyatta became Kenya's first African president (1964–1978) not unlike Nelson Mandela's presidency in South Africa in 1993.

Soon, Barack would be going on a merry-go-round of meeting relatives and friends. It was never-ending. He was squeezed and kissed by aunts and cousins until he could hardly catch his breath. Aunt Jane introduced him to Kezia, who was the mother of Auma and Roy, his half-sister and half brother.

There was talk about seeing Aunt Sarah, his father's sister. Barack could feel a wave of animosity rise against her because she was contesting his father's will and greedy for money. Auma told him that even her relatives were begging her for money since she had come from Germany.

Unlike the privacy factor in America, Barack's relatives in Kenya extended hospitality to him at every opportunity even when many were unemployed and did not have enough money. Auma had difficulty adjusting to Kenya society after living and prospering in Germany. She found herself taken advantage of by her relatives and risked their displeasure by declining many invitations. Barack was beginning to have the same feelings.

Finally, he visited Aunt Sarah, his father's sister, who complained that he should have visited her first. When he made the trip, she asked him for financial help. Reaching into his wallet, he gave her $30 in British money. He learned that his father had always been overgenerous, trying to help everyone in his family when he had nothing.

Then, there was an invitation from Ruth, his father's white, ex-wife. Her son Mark was attending Stanford University in Palo Alto, California. Ruth brought out her family album with photos of his father.

With these complex family divisions, Auma explained to Barack that divisions on the continent of Africa existed as well as in Kenya. These were tribal divisions.

Barack's reply, "It's thinking like that that holds us back. We're all part of one tribe. The black tribe. The human tribe."

After many discussions, Barack and his relatives made a trip by an overnight, colonial train that took them from Nairobi to a place near Alego, home of his grandfather, Hussein Onyango, to see Granny.

On the way, half-brother Roy described their grandfather as a terror, "Wow, that guy was mean! He would make you sit at the table for dinner, and served food on china, like an Englishman. If you said one wrong thing, or used the wrong fork—pow! He would hit you, you wouldn't even know why until the next day."

Aunt Zeitini, his father's sister, added more information, "Actually, he was well respected because he was such a good farmer. His compound in Alego was one of the biggest in the area. He had such a green thumb, he could make anything grow. He had studied these techniques from the British, you see, when he worked for them as a cook."

At Kisumu, they took a rickety, old bus to Ndori where a car met and drove them to Granny's hut. Inside the hut was his father's diploma from Harvard, proudly displayed on a wall. There were baby pictures of his father that young Barack looked at closely.

The meaning of his trip to Kenya and to his relatives was beginning to take shape, "It was simply joy that I felt in each of these moments. Rather, it was a sense that everything I was doing every touch and breath and word, carried the full weight of my life, that a circle was beginning to close, so that I might finally recognize myself as I was, here, now, in one place ... and I knew that at some point the joy I was feeling would pass and that that, too, was part of the circle."

Part of the circle was discovering his heritage through his grandfather and father. His grandfather had married a young girl, Akumu, from Kendu Lake, not far from Alego. Onyango was a very strict husband and a neat freak. Akumu was not happy and kept running away to her parents. Sarah and Barack were her two children. Eventually, she left Onyango for good and Onyango returned to Alego after returning from World War II.

Onyango, he learned, was delighted to find out how bright his son Barack was. The boy could outwit his teachers. He would drop out of school for weeks and then study for the exam for only three days and become the academic star of the class.

Even when Barack married Kezia and had a son, he was still restless for intellectual stimulation. Two American ladies in

Nairobi helped him get a school certificate, making him eligible to apply to twenty-six American universities. The University of Hawaii accepted him on scholarship. He left his wife and son behind for this new adventure. The rest of the story was familiar to Barack because his mother met his father at the University of Hawaii and married him.

Before leaving Kenya on this summer visit, Barack and his relatives dressed up for a family portrait to record their kinship with their American relative. Of the many vivid memories from his father's homeland, Barack would remember kneeling between the unmarked graves of his father and grandfather at twilight and letting the tears flow uncontrollably.

As the final days approached, Auma and Barack traveled by train from Nairobi to Mombasa, a coastal town on the Indian Ocean, where they walked and talked on a sandy beach along the blue-green waters.

On a bus ride back to Nairobi, Barack marveled at the sight of the famous baobab tree, framed against a dazzling sunset. Its branches clawed at the night sky like gnarled witches' fingers. This would be something he wouldn't forget.

As the wings of his airplane soared out of Kenya's International Airport, Barack Obama knew that his search for his roots and his identity had been found to give him peace within.

Now he could move on with his American life.

What would be his next experience?

Barack's father from Kenya

Barack's mother (Ann Dunham Obama)

Barack at ten-years-old with his father in the airport. This was the last time he saw his father.

The Soetoro family: Lolo, Ann, Maya, and Barack.

High School senior at Punahou School in Hawaii.

A brilliant student at Harvard University Law School.

Gramps (Stanley Dunham), Barack, and Tutu (Madelyn Dunham), Obama's grandparents.

Michelle, Barack's mother, and Barack at their wedding.

Michelle, Barack, Sasha, and Malia Obama, 2007.

The patriotic Barack Obama.

8

Attending Harvard University

Harvard University has the ring of reverence about it as one of the oldest colleges in the United States. The twenty-two acre Harvard Yard, enclosed by a series of tall wrought iron gates and fences, holds more than 370 years of history amid the crisscross of quadrangles and New England brick buildings (dating back to 1720) with white framed windows and white steeple spires. Art and history museums hug the perimeters of the campus.

Founded in 1636, the college was named after its benefactor, John Harvard, in 1638. Seven U.S. presidents and forty Nobel Prize winners graduated from this esteemed university. One such notable was poet Henry Wadsworth Longfellow (a graduate of Bowdoin College in Maine), who taught modern languages at Harvard. His house on Brattle Street is a historic site. Radcliffe College for women was established as part of Harvard in the 1870s. When it merged with Harvard between 1977 and 1999, discrimination between the sexes was erased.

The cheek of the Yard rubs against the throbbing Harvard Square in Cambridge, Massachusetts. The Square plays host to the famed Harvard Coop Bookstore, many banks, churches, a variety of ethnic restaurants, and some unique shops. Students swarm into the Square between classes for coffee and tasty tidbits. At night the Square is alive with young people wandering to and fro in joyous laughter or catching the subway (T) to downtown Boston. Within the Yard, Widener and Houghton Libraries are filled with students, intent on research, study, and learning as much as they can.

Barack Obama would follow his father's footsteps to Harvard, only his focus would be on law and not economics. The Harvard Law School, located outside the Yard to the north, had its own cluster of buildings from its founding in 1817. Only a select number of students were chosen. Out of 6,000 applications, a little over 500 were enrolled. They would be divided into seven sections of about 80 students in each section.

After three years as a Chicago community organizer and part of the summer in Kenya, Barack was ready to apply himself to serious study at Harvard Law School in the fall of 1988. His experience and maturity gave him purpose. His days of partying ended at Occidental College in Pasadena.

To work off stress and energy from intense study, Barack joined a group of law students to play his favorite sport in a Harvard gym—basketball. One time, the group divided themselves into two teams and began a game. Suddenly, there was a clash of bodies and tempers. To stop the fight, the tall, high-socked forward, Barack Obama, came off the bench to get between the two opponents.

He said, "Guys, this is not serious—it's just a pick-up game."

Earl Martin Phalen, a fellow classmate, added, "There was all this testosterone exploding and he just kind of had perspective … We ended up chilling out."

Obama stood out on the Law School campus. He wore his bomber jacket and faded jeans. Obviously, he was part of a small group of minorities, who were very ambitious.

This method of mediation, as witnessed in settling the basketball feud, was his attitude in law classes. He was a listener of other points of view. After hearing them, he would find a little from each side and put together a moderate compromise or solution.

For example, Obama moderated a debate on Affirmative Action. He drew out the conservatives, who wanted to abolish it, and admonished the liberals to produce a clearer, more convincing set of arguments. Never at any point did he inject his own views as a man of color.

In 1990 at 28-years-old, Barack Obama was the first black in its 104 year-old history to be elected President of the Harvard Law Review. Eighty editors made the selection. A flurry of excitement and attention erupted from the media, and Barack was the center of press coverage. Book contracts resulted from all the publicity.

When asked about his election to the Harvard Law Review, he said, "The fact that I've been elected shows a lot of progress. It's encouraging. But it's important that stories like mine aren't used to say that everything is O.K. for blacks. You have to remember that for every one of me, there are hundreds or thousands of black students with at least equal talent who don't get a chance."

"I personally am interested in pushing a strong minority perspective. I'm fairly opinionated about this. But as president of the law review, I have a limited role as only first among equals."

When law students protested against Harvard Law's discrimination and lack of diversity in the faculty, Obama would be supportive, but his eye was more on the goal than active protestation.

Except for his obsession with basketball and work at the Law Review, Obama was something of a loner and his social life on the back burner.

"I went to Harvard Law School, spending most of three years in poorly lit libraries, poring through cases and statutes. The study of law can be disappointing at times, a matter of applying narrow rules and arcane procedure to an uncooperative reality, a sort of glorified accounting that serves to regulate the affairs of those who have power—and that all too often seeks to explain, to those who do not, the ultimate wisdom and justness of their condition.

But that's not all the law is. The law is also memory; the law also records a long-running conversation, a nation arguing with its conscience."

Laurence H. Tribe, who taught Constitutional Law at Harvard, hired him as a research assistant. He claimed that in all his thirty-seven years of teaching, he had never found anyone as smart as this young man.

Barack Obama would graduate magna cum laude from Harvard Law School in 1991. A promising future was before him. Over 600 Wall Street firms wanted to hire him. He was offered a Supreme Court clerkship, but turned it down.

What was the reason he rejected these phenomenal opportunities?

9

Falling in Love

It was the summer after his first year at Harvard Law School that Barack Obama's personal life would change. He was anxious to find a job that would help pay his debts—student loans and day to day living expenses. The law firm of Sidley and Austin in Chicago hired him. Because this was a corporate law firm, Barack felt guilty about joining it since his three years as a community organizer had paid very little. Nevertheless, his need for a paycheck outweighed his guilt.

On the very first day, he met a tall, slender, and very bright young woman, who guided him through the details of the office layout. This was Michelle Robinson, who also went to Harvard Law School. This gave them an immediate connection.

Over a business lunch in the cafeteria, Barack extracted bits of personal information about Michelle. He found out that she had grown up on the South Side of Chicago, and she had graduated from Princeton University before going to Harvard Law School. For Princeton, she had played on the girls' basketball team. Their common interests were growing. Michelle was an expert in entertainment law and hoped to go to New York City or Los Angeles to practice her craft.

However, Michelle was careful not to mix business with personal associations in the office. In other words, she refused to go out on a date with Barack. Instead, she tried to match-make him with other young women.

Exasperated by her refusals, he threatened to resign from the law firm. Finally, she gave up her resistance. She accepted his invitation to sit on a street curb with him, licking an ice cream cone. This was their first date. A slow growing romance began over that summer. They saw each other every day and shared their life stories.

When Barack met her family, he was surprised to find them like a 1950s couple, raising two children. Michelle's mother, Marian, was a typical housewife, who baked big batches of cookies for her children and their friends. Her father, Frasier, was a pump operator, supporting his family. Her brother, Craig, was a tall, lanky basketball freak, who also graduated from Princeton, and was an investment banker.

The Robinsons, despite living in the poor section of Chicago, appeared to be the perfect American family. Barack had never had such a complete family unit growing up, except briefly in Indonesia when Lolo was his stepfather. Michelle's family was big. Cousins and relatives visited frequently, bringing laughter and music into the Robinson home.

And yet, tragedy was mixed with joy. The Robinsons had to face racial discrimination, but they were to face an even bigger personal challenge. Frasier Robinson contracted Multiple Sclerosis at the early age of thirty. He never complained about his deteriorating condition. At first he had a limp and then he used two canes to get to work, but he adjusted his time schedule to allow for dressing. With these added difficulties, Marian started working part-time in a bank like Barack's grandmother had in Hawaii.

The devastating news of his death after six months of meeting Michelle hit Barack very hard. He flew back from Cambridge to Chicago to pay his respects at the funeral and to support Michelle and her grieving family. Barack remembered his feelings when news of his own father's death in Kenya from an automobile accident was delivered to him in a telephone call from a relative. He knew the desperate emptiness that Michelle must be experiencing. When a parent passes away, there is an irreplaceable loss and a realization that one would be going forward alone without a parent to turn to or to share a family joke. It would be a new chapter for her as it had been for him.

The following summer, Barack and Michelle became engaged. They traveled to Hawaii to meet Toot and Gramps, who were impressed with Michelle's intellect and attractive appearance. The newly engaged couple also flew to Kenya to meet all the Obamas. Michelle even learned some phrases in Luo to communicate with the relatives.

Once Barack graduated Magna Cum Laude from Harvard Law School, wedding plans were made for Michelle and Barack. Reverend Wright from Trinity United Church of Christ performed the ceremony. Barack's mother was there as well as many of his friends from Chicago and Kenya. Michelle's relatives were there in full force.

Now a married man, Barack joined a small law firm, devoted to civil rights. He even found time to teach Constitutional Law at the University of Chicago.

Like all married couples, there were adjustments. Michelle was an early morning person and Barack, a night person. Michelle discovered that Barack could be quite grumpy in the morning, and he was forgetful about little things—like putting the butter back in the fridge after breakfast. These are all admissions made honestly by Barack in his book, *Audacity of Hope.*

Would Barack's ambitions take him beyond life in a law firm?

10

State Senator for Illinois

The fire for politics must have been burning in Obama's soul before and during his years at Harvard University. Apparently, he talked among his Harvard friends about the possibility of running for political office in his state of Illinois after he graduated with a law degree.

Perhaps his years as a community organizer opened his eyes, pointing him in the direction of law and politics as the two ways to get things done in helping average people of all races, but particularly those of color, to find jobs and some kind of future for black youth mired in despair. It would take patience and hard work.

Because of Barack's notoriety at Harvard as the first African American to become president of the Harvard Law Review publication, he had signed a contract for $1.9 million to write three books. The first one was an autobiography, called *Dreams from my Father.* For anyone who has ever written a book, this takes time and solitude. Newly married and employed by Miner, Barnhill, and Galland to work on civil discrimination cases, Barack's life didn't leave much time for leisure while writing the book.

Once the book deadline was met, he continued to teach Constitutional Law at the University of Chicago at night and work at the law firm during the day. He and Michelle rarely saw each other in the hustle to build their careers.

However, the desire to enter politics was never very far from his thoughts. Finally, in 1996 he decided to take the plunge. Before launching into a campaign, he ran the idea by Michelle. Her reaction was surprising. She thought it was a crazy idea because he would be commuting every week between Chicago and Springfield, Illinois, where the state capitol was located. Going by car or bus would take three or four hours. By plane, it would only take forty minutes, but the cost would be much higher. Although not thrilled by her husband's dream, Michelle weakened and gave her support.

Therefore, Barack Obama began campaigning for state senator in the 13th District on the south side of Chicago, which included the Hyde Park section, where poverty and racial tensions existed. He was familiar with the needs and frustrations of the people he wanted to represent. He had made many friends there as a community organizer, which probably was a factor in his winning the election. In the campaign process, people told him to change his name and downplay his African heritage from Kenya.

This was Barack Obama's response, "Now all of this may be good political advice, but it's all so superficial. I am surprised at how many elected officials—even the good ones—spend so much time talking about the mechanics of politics and not matters of substance."

Obama's whole belief was in giving communities empowerment to build their destinies.

His successor to the Developing Communities Project as executive director, Johnnie Owens, made this observation about

Obama, "He brought a certain level of sophistication and intelligence to community work … He's not about calling attention to himself. He's concerned with the work. It's as if it's his mission in life, his calling, to work for social justice."

Because American society is obsessed with the importance of the individual, this is Obama's response, "In America we have this strong bias toward individual action. You know, we idolize the John Wayne hero who comes in to correct things with both guns and blazing. But individual actions, individual dreams, are not sufficient. We must unite in collective action, build collective institutions and organizations."

To his voters, he said this, "But cursing out white folks is not going to get the job done. Anti-Semitic and anti-Asian statements are not going to lift us up. We've got some hard nuts and bolts organizing and planning to do. We've got communities to build."

Barack would win the senate election and head to Springfield early in 1997 for the legislative session. His high ideals were embedded in his heart and mind, and he hoped somehow he could make a difference.

Springfield oozes with historic charm. When Barack arrived, the handsome Abraham Lincoln Presidential Library had not been built in its magnificent Egyptian limestone. That would come in 2004. Unlike Chicago, Barack found the center of Springfield to be small and laid out on the grid system. Harsh winters most likely caused the buildings to be placed within walking distance of each other.

The old 1839 State Capitol, the Lincoln Home National Historic Site, and the 1840 Lincoln-Herndon Law Offices (William R. Herndon was Lincoln's law partner, but also his biographer) draw visitors and tourists to Springfield. The Lincoln Tomb, set among rolling hills and flanked by pink and white dogwood trees in the Oak Ridge Cemetery, is only ten minutes from downtown and a fascinating architectural wonder.

Surrounded by this historic atmosphere, Senator Obama would attend senate sessions in the impressive new State Capitol (built in the 1870s) on 2nd Street and Capitol Street. The building had been built in an ornate, French Renaissance style. Inside is a rotunda of beige—almost peach-like marble where the click of leather shoes and high heels echo to the dome above. On each floor are wrought iron balustrades and arched niches for statues. The Governor's office has modern glass and marble.

Located on the third floor of the north wing, the senate chamber, during Obama's term, for fifty-nine members had heavy walnut wood walls, a red carpet, and red leather chairs with the state seal on the head rest. Today, those chairs are brown leather with the seal at the back and the chamber is much lighter and brighter.

Usually, the sessions are from January to the end of May and sometimes into July. The order of business is to enact, amend, and repeal laws. Resolutions, inquiries, and proposed legislation are discussed in committees and brought before the senate and house.

Senator Obama called Emil Jones, the Illinois state president, his "political godfather." Jones supported and encouraged the youthful politician. He noticed how comfortable he was in moving among all peoples, such as blacks, Hispanics, and whites—rich or poor.

During the first few years of Obama's arrival, the Republicans were in the majority. Democrats had a hard time passing their bills. Furthermore, Obama faced political prejudice from both sides because of his handsome appearance and easy command of language, which provoked envy among his colleagues. Unaware of these undercurrents, Barack reached out to Republicans and Democrats to find common ground on issues. He persisted and persuaded with untold patience.

But his job as state senator was an opportunity to put into practice his deep held beliefs. Passing bills was the way to do it. Out of 780 bills presented during his eight years, 280 were passed, in which he had personal involvement.

Although sarcasm and ridicule were not his style, Obama related an incident, causing him to respond to his opponent partly with humor and partly with seriousness.

Apparently, a Republican was debating against providing breakfasts to preschoolers. His flimsy argument said, "… it would crush their spirit of self-reliance."

Obama couldn't resist saying, "… not too many five-year-olds I know are self-reliant, but children who spent their formative years too hungry to learn could very well end up as being charges of the state." Despite some sympathetic laughter, the bill did not pass until a different version was passed.

One way Obama found to make friends with both party members was to play poker with them. It broke the ice and gained the admiration of his colleagues and opponents.

Republican Kirk Dillard said, "… Obama impressed with his work ethic and commitment to getting things done … He'll show up at any meeting that requires his attention."

Suddenly in 2000, Obama wanted a broader canvas for his ideas and perhaps he was impatient to have a wider audience to hear them. Whatever the inner reasons, he decided to run for U.S. Congressman for Illinois against the man who was up for re-election—Bobby Rush. Rush was popular and Obama had an eleven percent chance of winning. Rush defeated him and Obama suffered the burning feeling of being a loser. It hurt, but he learned some lessons about running for office and what he needed to do before announcing a campaign on that scale.

On the heels of this defeat, he and his family went to Hawaii on vacation to visit his grandparents and his mother. A call from Springfield indicated there was a critical vote on gun control, and it was necessary for him to return to cast his vote. His daughter became critically ill, and he couldn't leave. The press slaughtered him for living the good life in Hawaii and not giving up his vacation to come back to vote. The gun control vote was defeated by a few votes.

During his eight years in the Illinois state senate, there were some key bills that he was responsible for passing:

a. Earned Income Tax Credit for lower income families.

b. Early Childhood education.

c. Health Insurance for those who couldn't afford it.

d. AIDS prevention and cure.

e. Insurance companies required to cover routine mammograms for women.

f. Stop mortgage lenders from charging outrageous rates to low-income homeowners.

Probably his most important piece of legislation was a requirement for the police to videotape their interrogations and confessions of criminals who might be subject to the death penalty. Obama's purpose for this bill was "to convict the guilty as well as save the innocent." He also wanted confessions to be freely given and not forced.

Perhaps the highlight of his state senate career was a speech in October of 2002 when he took a positive stand against going to war in Iraq. The actual war did not begin until March of 2003, but the rumblings and talk of war by the administration and Republicans were well underway a year before the attack was made. False intelligence from the CIA and speeches made at the United Nations held Americans hostage to the idea for pursuing an invasion of Iraq.

Obama claimed that the war in Iraq was a wrong concept and that Iraq's leader, Saddam Hussein, was not a present threat to the United States. He warned that the invasion of Iraq would lead to occupation of that country for an undetermined length of time.

Here are Obama's words in that 2002 speech:

"I don't oppose wars … What I am opposed to is a dumb war. What I am opposed to is a rash war." Those words and warnings would be appealing to his presidential voters in 2007.

What would his next career move be?

11

Kids and United States Senator

According to almost every parent, children are an amazing gift to the world and to each family. Michelle and Barack Obama welcomed their two daughters with that indescribable feeling, which new birth brings.

Malia arrived in 1999. During that first summer when she was only a few months old, her parents doted, cooed, and sang little songs to her over those hot days and weeks. Both parents had a breather from their busy work schedules, allowing them the luxury of giving undivided attention to their baby.

Sasha was born in 2001, adding a sister for Malia and another precious daughter to the Obama family unit. Barack's time was not as available for Sasha as it had been for Malia, but his devotion to his family was never in question. The absence of his own father from his childhood and life was ever a reminder of his responsibility to his two girls.

However, the fire in his belly and inner restlessness for politics was still burning. When Obama decided to run for U.S. senator for Illinois, Michelle was even more skeptical than she had been when he ran for state senator.

Full of confidence, Barack told Michelle, "… I'm going to win the primary, the general, and then, I'm going to write a book."

Unconvinced, Michelle reluctantly gave her support because she realized that her husband was unstoppable.

The shocking event of 9/11 had a devastating effect on Obama's future political career. His name was very close to that of Osama bin Laden, leader of the radical group Al Qaeda, determined to bring down America and its people.

The prospect of running against Republican Peter Fitzgerald, who was rich and well connected, would be an uphill battle. Then, Fitzgerald dropped out of the race, leaving six Democrats in the running for the primary election.

Furthermore, the Illinois senate was good training ground for a young man, whose eyes were set on the white capitol building in the cherry blossom district, lining the banks of the Potomac River, in Washington, D.C.

Like a football or baseball game, there are two teams—the Republicans and the Democrats. Each team wants to win by persuasion, distraction, or outright aggression, using rough and tumble tactics. Sometimes honey-coated flattery would work and sometimes doses of vinegar would work. Obama was learning the game of politics hopefully without sacrificing his integrity.

On a hot July night in 2004, presidential candidate John Kerry, Democratic senator from Massachusetts, invited Barack Obama to give the keynote address at the Democratic Convention in Boston. The young politician moved out of obscurity into the limelight of political center stage.

The television audience found him refreshing and found his ideas resonating with them. He stole the thunder from John Kerry as Ronald Reagan had done at the 1964 Republican Convention when he gave the keynote address for Barry Goldwater.

Reagan's phrase, "We have a rendezvous with destiny" became the national buzz. Obama's phrase "for unity and hope" also caught the attention of Americans, fatigued by the same old political rhetoric. Even President and Mrs. George W. Bush were impressed.

Obama's wealthy Republican, political opponent for the U.S. Senate seat from Illinois had to drop out of the race because of a personal scandal. To replace him, the Republicans uprooted the articulate Ph. D. from Harvard, Alan Keyes from Maryland, to oppose Obama in Illinois. This decision was made after the convention speech. Obama talked to voters all over Illinois and won their favor. He knew them. Keyes didn't. Obama had lived in Illinois and Keyes hadn't. He had listened to the people of Illinois. Keyes talked at them and was on a bashing Barack mission. Keyes didn't know the basic wants of families for their kids and for the environment or for retirement. Obama did.

Despite all that, Keyes proved to be an annoying rival for Obama. He had hired a young man to film Obama's every move with a video camera. He wouldn't go away. He was always around. Finally, the press picked up on it, making hot copy for reporters and cartoonists.

Even in politics, Obama lives by the Golden Rule and he finds it an obligation to see what it must be like to stand in someone else's shoes.

Fundraising was the hardest. The only way to pay for TV ads was to ask rich people to contribute huge amounts. To get big money, Obama had to spend more time with rich folks.

He defeated Keyes and won the election to the U.S. Senate. It was a sweet victory. And he was on the path of doing what he wanted—being useful.

When Senator Barack Obama arrived in D.C. as number 99 out of 100 senators, he found his tiny office in the basement of the Dirksen Office Building. He called a press conference. No one had space to move. His first question on his first day was this, "Senator Obama, what is your place in history?" Laughter from everyone, including the junior senator, was the answer. The buzz he created at the Democratic Convention was still buzzing.

In January 2005, the Democrats were still in the minority in both the House of Representatives and the Senate. Therefore, they welcomed the junior senator from Illinois as a good sign of victory for the future. By the 2006 election, the tables had turned and the Democrats were no longer losers. They had recaptured both houses. The public had become disenchanted with President George W. Bush and his foreign policy; particularly in Iraq.

Obama was sworn into the halls of Congress in January of 2005 when the Republicans were savoring their 2004 presidential victory for a second term.

Within days, Obama was casting his first vote to install George W. Bush as president. Within moments of that vote, his telephone wouldn't stop ringing. His Illinois voters were angry over the voting procedures in Ohio, and they wanted an investigation. Obama agreed that an investigation had to go forward, although he was convinced President Bush had won the election.

Bitter division between the two parties was very apparent to the junior senator. He questioned older members about the bad feelings. They replied that they longed for the days when there was bipartisanship and at the end of the day, opponents would put aside politics and go to dinner together. For two decades that had not been the case.

During Obama's first few months on Capitol Hill, he felt like he was spinning in a whirlpool. There were hundreds of letters from his constituents, committee assignments, becoming acquainted with issues, and piles of paperwork.

Most of all, Barack Obama sorely missed his wife and young family. They had decided to stay in Chicago while he commuted weekends from his small apartment in D.C.

He used the time away from his family to concentrate on his senatorial duties. Because of his new star power, he received 250 to 500 requests a week to speak. Instead, he used his time to lobby for aid for Darfur at the United Nations.

Obama focused his attention on public education, ethics, economic growth and jobs as well as on the Iraq War.

As a freshman senator in the 109th Congress, he visited esteemed members such as Senator Robert C. Byrd of West Virginia and Senator Edward M. Kennedy of Massachusetts for advice to a newcomer. Byrd recommended learning the rules of the senate and the constitution. Byrd told him that the constitution and the Holy Bible were his two guides in life.

In the 110th Congress, Senator Obama was assigned to seven committees. They were: Foreign Relations; African Affairs; Subcommittee for International Economic Policy; Subcommittee for Asians and Pacific Affairs; Committee on Veterans' Affairs; Committee on Health, Education, Labor, and Pensions; and the Committee for Homeland Security and Government Affairs.

With two young daughters, the Senator had a great interest in education. He accepted an invitation to speak before American Librarians on June 27, 2005.

"Right now, children come home from their first doctor's appointment with an extra bottle of formula. But imagine if they came home with their first library card or their first copy of 'Goodnight Moon.' What if it was easy to get a book as it is to rent a DVD or pick up at McDonalds? What if instead of a toy in every Happy Meal, there was a book? What if there were portable libraries that rolled through parks and playgrounds like ice cream trucks? Or kiosks in stores where you could borrow books.

What if during the summer when kids often lose much of the reading progress they've made during the year, every child had a list of books they had to read and talk about and an invitation to a summer reading club at the local library? Librarians have a special role to play in our knowledge economy."

In the U.S. Senate, Obama sponsored ninety-one bills, but only one passed—to promote relief, security, and democracy in the Democratic Republic of the Congo in December of 2006. He voted with his party 96 or 97% of the time. Only twenty-four bills make it to the senate floor for a vote in a year.

When he offered a "present" vote, it was like a "no" vote, but was used as a political cover when he didn't want to commit himself on the vote.

Here were some amendments that Senator Obama was able to get passed:

"We helped provide funds for homeless veterans. We provided tax credits to gas stations for installing E85 fuel pumps. We obtained funding to help the World Health Organization monitor and respond to a potential avian flu pandemic. We got an amendment out of the Senate elimination no-bid contracts in the post-Katrina reconstruction, so more money would actually end up in the hands of the tragedy's victims."

Along with committee work, Senator Obama occasionally attended prayer breakfasts on Wednesday mornings when Republicans and Democrats would share their spiritual journeys.

On Thursday mornings, Barack Obama and his fellow senator from Illinois met with residents from their state if they dropped into the D.C. office to discuss issues. They served coffee and doughnuts. Because of Obama's popularity, they had to move the Thursday morning meetings to a larger room to accommodate 150 people. The nickname "Healer-in-Chief" was given to him.

One of his proudest moments was his collaboration with Republican Richard Lugar, who was Chairman of the Senate Foreign Relations Committee. The two men joined forces to sponsor a piece of legislation to restrict weapons proliferation and black-market arms trade. They had reached across the aisle and across party lines for the good of the American people.

◆   ◆   ◆

In between his first and second session of the Senate, Senator Obama, his wife, and two daughters traveled to Kenya during the summer recess of 2006 to introduce his girls to their paternal grandfather's heritage.

This time, his greeting was very different. A United States Ambassador met the family at the airport. Lines of Kenyans waited to catch a glimpse of him with signs, calling him their "brother" or "son."

The family went to the village where Barack's father and grandfather were buried. Even there, Obama was treated like a hero with singing and gifts. One villager even wanted to give him a goat, but Obama told him diplomatically that he had to decline his kind gift. His half-sister Auma was there to translate from Luo to English.

In a short speech, Obama said, "I felt the spirit among the people who told me that I belonged."

The question is what does Barack Obama believe? What is his philosophy of life?

12

His Philosophy

Over a period of years, this young man had begun to formulate his own ideas about politics, his personal philosophy, and thoughts about the subject of race, which he addressed eloquently in his book *Audacity of Hope.*

Although Senator Obama is a dedicated Democrat, he does not demonize the Republican President. He attacks his policies or the administration. People are surprised when Obama announces that George W. Bush is not a bad man.

"... after all the trappings of office—the titles, the staff, the security details—are stripped away, I find the President and those who surround him to be pretty much like everybody else, possessed of the same mix of virtues and vices, insecurities, and long-buried injuries, as the rest of us. No matter how wrong-headed I might consider their policies to be—and no matter how much I might insist they be held accountable ... I still find it possible, in talking to these men and women to understand their motives and to recognize in them values I share."

Although this may seem a strange point of view, Obama's training as a lawyer gives him the capacity to look at all sides and to separate opposing opinions from the individual.

Obama cites the Declaration of Independence as a prized document, giving individual freedom to each American.

The reason the Senator feels strongly about the Bill of Rights may stem from his boyhood years in Indonesia where military dictatorship prevailed, restricting individual freedoms. Furthermore, his three overseas visits to Kenya revealed internal corruption and bribery as a way of life. He observed that liberty brings personal responsibility as well as free will.

"But these values also express a broader confidence so long as individual men and women are free to pursue their own interests, society as a whole will prosper. Our system of self-government and our free market economy depend on the majority of individual Americans adhering to these values."

Here, Obama points out the things that we value in this country: family, community, patriotism, faith, and respect.

Respect for others is one of his core values. Perhaps that comes from his bi-racial heritage and from straddling two worlds—the black world and the white world. He moves easily between both.

Good manners rank high as another basic value. And he admires competence in whatever endeavor.

Obama doesn't believe in censorship, but he believes in constraints. For example, certain television programs are unsuitable for children and he believes there should be constraints on them.

Shakespeare's line, "To thine own self be true" is a line applied directly to his own philosophy. Obama tries to be himself and not an actor in politics. "… The quality of authenticity of being who you say you are, of possessing a truthfulness that goes beyond words … Perhaps this explains why we long for that most elusive quality in our leaders—the quality of authenticity."

The most revealing quality of Obama's character is empathy, which he learned from his fellow Illinois Senator Paul Simon and from his own mother, Ann Dunham Obama Soetoro.

"The last aspect of Paul's (Simon) character—a sense of empathy—is one that I find myself appreciating more and more as I get older. It is at the heart of my moral code, and it is how I understand the Golden Rule—not simply as a call to sympathy or charity, but as something more demanding, a call to stand in somebody else's shoes and see through their eyes."

From his mother, there were strong lessons. "She disdained any kind of cruelty or thoughtlessness or abuse of power, whether it expressed itself in the form of racial prejudice or bullying in the schoolyard or workers being underpaid. Whenever she saw even a hint of such behavior in me, she would look me square in the eyes and ask, 'How do you think that would make you feel?'"

During Barack's teenage years in Hawaii, he would often get into arguments with his grandfather over certain rules imposed on him. "I recognized that sometimes he really did have a point, and that insisting on getting my own way all the time, without regard to his feelings or needs, I was in some way diminishing myself."

"… I find myself returning again and again to my mother's simple principle—'How would that make you feel?'—as a guidepost for my politics." Barack Obama's mother died of cancer in 1995.

Since Obama himself has a mixed racial lineage of black and white, he also has in-laws of Indonesian and Chinese descent. His half-sister Maya is of Indonesian and white heritage.

"I've never had the option of restricting my loyalties on the basis of race or measuring my worth on the basis of tribe … I believe that part of America's genius has always been the ability to absorb newcomers, to forge a national identity out of the disparate lot that arrived on our shores."

The reason Barack Obama has become such a rising star is one quotable statement from the 2004 Convention. "There is not a black America and white America and Latino America and Asian America—there's the United States of America."

Realistically, Obama is aware that racial prejudice still exists, but not to the degree it once did. Today, there are black mayors of white communities across the country.

Obama himself has been the object of prejudice. "… security guards tailing me as I shop in department stores, white couples who toss me their car keys as I stood outside a restaurant for the valet, police cars pulling me over for no apparent reason … I know the bitter swill of swallowed black anger."

Probably the two major issues that bring the Senator the most criticism are his pro-choice stand on abortion and the gay rights issue. Many devout Christians have challenged his positions.

"… I explained my belief that few women made the decision to terminate a pregnancy casually; that any pregnant woman felt the full force of the moral issues involved and wrestled with her conscience when making that heart-wrenching decision; that I feared a ban on abortion would force a woman to seek unsafe abortions … I suggested that perhaps we could agree on ways to reduce the number of women who felt the need to have an abortion in the first place."

His view on gays and civil unions for gays was changed dramatically when a very dear friend and supporter left a message on his telephone machine, expressing her disappointment on his objection to gays. She admitted to him that she was a lesbian and had been in a longtime relationship. Obama had to reconsider his ideas. He now supports civil unions, but not marriage for gays.

"I am not willing to have the state deny America citizens a civil union that confers equivalent rights on such basic matters as hospital visitation or health insurance coverage simply because the people they love are of the same sex ..."

As for his own religious faith, Barack Obama has been on a long spiritual journey. He has settled on the Trinity United Church of Christ in Chicago, but he allows himself the freedom to question and to explore spiritual issues in his own mind.

What would be his next step in the political world?

13

Running for President in 2008

Ever since Barack Obama hit the Senate in 2005, he became an instant celebrity. His lanky frame, striking good looks, baritone voice, and gift for speech-making have put him in a Hollywood category, unlike any other politician, except perhaps John F. Kennedy.

His 2004 speech at the Democratic convention catapulted him into political stardom. Wherever he turned, members of the public from both parties encouraged him to enter the 2008 political race for president. His words about "a <u>United</u> States of America" have resonated across the country.

By the summer and fall of 2006, Obama was beginning to sound more and more like a presidential candidate.

One of his biggest assets is his wife, Michelle. This Princeton and Harvard graduate is the Senator's anchor and provides a dose of reality to his life. She is totally honest about her marriage and everything.

Following her husband's footsteps, Michelle left her corporate law firm in 1991 in exchange for public service. First, she was an assistant to the mayor and then, she became assistant commissioner of planning and development for the City of Chicago. Next, she moved to a leadership training program, helping young adults learn skills, preparing them for work in the public sector. By 1996 she was associate dean of student services at the University of Chicago.

With her growing family of two daughters, Michelle Obama adjusted her schedule to become vice president of community and external affairs at the University of Chicago Hospital and its diversity of programs.

Just before Barack Obama stepped into the limelight at the 2004 Democratic Convention in Boston, Michelle hugged him backstage and whispered into his ear, "Don't screw it up, buddy." He didn't. He created buzz, and the buzz hasn't stopped.

Here are some excerpts from that famous seventeen minute speech:

"Tonight, we gather to affirm the greatness of our nation—not because of the height of our skyscrapers, or the power of our military, or the size of our economy. Our pride is based on a very simple premise, summed up in a declaration made two hundred years ago: 'We hold these truths to be self-evident, that all men are created equal, that they are endowed by their Creator with certain unalienable rights, that among these are life, liberty, and the pursuit of happiness.'

That is the true genius of American—a faith in simple dreams, an insistence on small miracles."

"People don't expect government to solve all their problems. But they sense, deep in their bones, that with just a slight change in priorities, we can make sure that every child in America has a decent shot at life, and that the doors of opportunity remain open to all."

"… It is that fundamental belief—that I am my brother's keeper, I am my sister's keeper—that makes this country work."

"… Hope in the face of difficulty. Hope in the face of uncertainty. The audacity of hope! In the end, that is God's greatest gift to us, the bedrock of this nation. A belief in things not seen. A belief that there are better days ahead."

By February 2007, Senator Obama was ready to announce his decision to run for president of the United States. The place he chose to launch his campaign was the capitol of Illinois, Springfield. Here, at the age of 21, Abraham Lincoln came from Kentucky and Indiana to serve as a self-taught lawyer, state representative, and congressman for a period of thirty years.

Under this umbrella of history, Barack Obama stood in front of the Old State Capitol building on 6th Street, where Abraham Lincoln delivered his famous "House Divided" speech. The Old Capitol was built in 1839 and was made of a rusty beige dolomite limestone. Inside, the ladder-like stairs go up to the senate chamber, and the wood stoves on the main floor burn all day to heat the building in winter.

On February 10, Barack, Michelle, and their two daughters stood, shivering, while the Senator delivered a twenty minute speech to almost 20,000 supporters. Michelle had finally surrendered to her husband's messianic desire to change his country by running for president.

Here are some highlights from that speech:

"… in the shadow of the Old State Capitol, where Lincoln once called on a divided house to stand together, with common hopes and common dreams still, I stand before you today to announce my candidacy for President of the United States. I recognize there is a certain presumptuousness—a certain audacity—to this announcement. I know I haven't spent a lot of time, learning the ways of Washington. But I've been there long enough to know that the ways of Washington must change.

It was here we learned to disagree without being disagree-able—that it's possible to compromise so long as you know those principles that can never be compromised, and that so long as we're willing to listen to each other, we can assume the best of people instead of the worst.

That's what Abraham Lincoln understood. He had his doubts. He had his defeats. He had his setbacks ... he moved a nation and helped free a people.

Let us be the generation that reshapes our economy to com-pete in the digital age ... Let's recruit a new army of teachers and give them better pay ... Let's make college more affordable ... and let's invest in scientific research ..."

"Let's be the generation that finally tackles our health care crisis ... Most of all let's be the generation that never forgets what happened on that September day and control the terrorists with everything we've got. Politics doesn't divide us on this any-more—we can work together to keep our country safe."

"That's why this campaign can't only be about me. It must be about us ... of your hopes and dreams."

"Together, starting today, let us finish the work that needs to be done, and usher in a new birth of freedom on this earth."

◆   ◆   ◆

From Michigan to Texas and from Cape Cod to California, Barack Obama and his family have carried the essence of the above message to voters, including healthcare for all. He raised large amounts of money from ordinary voters to corporations and from wealthy individuals to Hollywood producers and stars. Famed television talk-show host, Oprah Winfrey, gave a glamorous fundraiser for Obama at her California estate in September of 2007, raising three million dollars for his campaign. Senator John Kerry of Massachusetts, a Democratic presidential candidate in 2004, chose to give Obama his endorsement over that of his former running mate, Senator John Edwards.

By the end of August 2007, distinguished statesman, Zbigniew Brzezinski, President Jimmy Carter's former National Security Advisor, climbed aboard the Obama bandwagon and threw his full support behind the Illinois senator for president because of his unconventional ideas for solving global issues. Brzezinski felt that Hillary Clinton represented old, conventional ways of dealing with foreign policy.

In her own political quest, Senator Hillary Clinton was battling to become the first woman president. She knew her biggest threat would be from Obama because of his personal appeal and magnetism for voters. Although Senator Clinton remained ahead temporarily in the polls, Obama seesawed between first and second. In the early stages of the campaign, they exercised restraint from attacking each other in debates or on the campaign trail. At other times, their debates were heated and often left Senator John Edwards on the sidelines.

Of all the candidates from both parties, Obama drew the largest crowds. They were partly curious, but interested to hear his message.

He continued to badger the administration about withdrawing from Iraq. His plan insisted on bringing brigades (composed of 1,500 to 3,500 personnel) out by March 31, 2008 and the rest of the troops by the end of 2008. Of course, that never happened.

Here is his Iraq plan from a policy speech on September 12, 2007.

- Remove our combat troops from Iraq's civil war by the end of 2008.

- Take a new approach to press for reconciliation within Iraq.

- Escalate our diplomacy with all of Iraq's neighbors and the United Nations.

- Confront the human costs of this war directly with increased humanitarian aid.

On a minor note, the African/American community wondered whether Obama was black enough because of his white mother married to an African from Kenya.

Michelle Obama squashed that argument by saying, "Stop that nonsense!"

The other major hurdle Obama faced was the repeated question about his youth and inexperience. Obama's answer referred to Vice-President Richard Cheney and former Secretary of Defense, Donald Rumsfeld, as having the longest resumes in D.C. He implied that wisdom doesn't necessarily accompany maturity. Michelle waged a strong argument to stop those accusations about his inexperience.

Harvard University's Constitutional Law professor, Laurence H. Tribe gave a hearty response, "It's the quality, rather than the quantity, of experience that matters."

In most of 2007, all the candidates covered New Hampshire, Iowa, South Carolina, and Florida to rally support for early primary elections in January and February of 2008. In September of 2007, Obama conducted "faith forums" in Iowa where people could discuss faith, values, and politics.

However, he focused on three prime issues: Iraq, health care, and taxes. His views on the Iraq War have been evident since 2002.

In May of 2007, the Senator laid out a comprehensive plan for universal health care for all Americans. He condemned the high costs and bemoaned the fact that 57 million Americans (including children) don't have health insurance.

The Obama proposal offered affordable healthcare for everyone; a plan to hold costs in check and improve quality; emphasis on prevention of diseases; to provide federal subsidies; allow workers to keep health coverage while moving from job to job; and to establish a National Health Insurance Exchange.

With regard to taxes, Obama wanted to simplify the tax code and filing methods for the middle class. He warned companies against illegal abuses and consequences for violating the law. In a broad statement, he told voters that he wanted to cut taxes for the working class, homeowners, and seniors.

In the Iowa caucus on January 4, 2008, Obama won an upset victory over Hillary Clinton and John Edwards. Edwards came in second and Senator Clinton, a close third. Although he lost the New Hampshire primary to Hillary Clinton, he scored a resounding victory in South Carolina.

Inspired by Obama's broad appeal to Americans of all ages, Senator Edward Kennedy endorsed him as his choice for the Democratic presidential nomination in late January of 2008. Caroline Kennedy also gave her endorsement because she felt Obama's political character was closest to that of her father.

On the super Tuesday primaries of February 5, 2008, Clinton and Obama were neck and neck with Hillary finishing with more delegates. Senator John McCain took a major lead in the Republican primaries. By mid-February, Obama began to sweep more primaries and edged ahead of Clinton with delegates. During the March 4 primaries in Ohio and Texas, Senator Clinton moved, ever so slightly, ahead of Barack Obama. Nevertheless, Obama still held a substantial lead with delegates. He secured victories and delegates in Wyoming and Mississippi.

Inflammatory remarks from Obama's pastor in Chicago made Obama walk a diplomatic tightrope in distancing himself from Reverend Jeremiah Wright's political ideas, expressed in the pulpit during the start of Obama's campaign, but which surfaced on YouTube in March of 2008. The pastor has since retired. Obama characteristically refused to reject Wright as a longtime family friend. Following the dozens of television replays of Wright's remarks, Obama made a speech about race that was a classic and will remain memorable in the annals of history.

Unfortunately, Reverend Wright made various television appearances that continued to embarrass Obama at the end of April 2008. Senator Obama held a press conference to contradict, point by point, his opposing views. Some observers felt that the pastor might have damaged the public's perception of Obama's capacity for good judgment.

Hillary Clinton also had to distance herself from Geraldine Ferraro, who made some harsh racial remarks about Obama. Questions about Senator Clinton's involvement in foreign policy decisions during her husband's administration have arisen and also have come under close scrutiny. The findings described her participation as more ceremonial than in actual policy-making.

Bill Richardson, former U.S. Secretary of Energy during the Clinton administration and present Governor of New Mexico, endorsed Barack Obama despite longtime ties with the Clintons. He felt that Obama was a fresh new voice for change and could unify the country.

Furthermore, revelations from the State Department about employees breaking into passport records of Obama, Clinton, and McCain aroused further questions.

By the end of March 2008, the candidates were focusing on the economy, which experienced wide swings. Obama had been advised by the wizard investor, Warren Buffet, on a range of economic issues.

However, should Senator Obama and Senator Clinton continue with personal attacks, they could be in danger of turning the public away from both of them and into voting for the Republican nominee, Senator John McCain.

Also, at the end of March, a number of Democrats were calling for Senator Clinton to remove herself from the campaign. She refused and Obama generously said that she should continue even though he had won most of the popular vote and delegates.

Only days before the Pennsylvania primary on April 22, Obama made a remark in California about the workers in Pennsylvania as being "bitter" and "clinging to their religion and guns." Hillary Clinton seized on those remarks to her political advantage. She won the primary by ten points.

Despite his struggles, Obama won the North Carolina primary on May 6 by a wide margin and came within two points of beating Clinton in Indiana. The numbers indicated that eventually he would become the Democratic nominee.

Whether Barack Obama wins the 2008 Democratic nomination and election or not, his future has infinite possibilities. He could be chosen as a vice president or for a cabinet post or remain as a senator or be appointed to the Supreme Court or run again for president in 2012. Richard Nixon and Ronald Reagan both ran twice and won on the second try.

Barack Obama's desire for change and his audacity of hope have inspired millions of war-weary Americans during a period of disillusionment with politics and politicians.

He will find his niche either in the Oval Office or in another prestigious place of influence.

What is most memorable about Barack Obama? His character: his honesty, his trustworthiness, and his superior intellect. He has the ability to persuade a bitter enemy to become his best friend. That's why he is nicknamed "Healer in Chief."

Bibliography

Books

Brill, Marlene Targ. *Barack Obama: Working to make a difference.* Millbrook Press, Minneapolis. 2006.

Dougherty, Steve. *Hopes and Dreams: The Story of Barack Obama.* Black Dog and Leventhal Publishers, New York. 2007.

Obama, Barack. *Dreams of My Father.* Three Rivers Press, New York. 1995.

Obama, Barack. *The Audacity of Hope.* Crown Publishers, New York. 2006.

Zimmerman, Frederick W. *Should Barack Obama Be President?* Nimble Books, Ann Arbor. 2006.

Internet

www,barackobama.com

www.boston.com

www.bnd.com

www.chicagoreader.com

www.ilstatehouse.com/senate

www.keithboykin.com (January 2007)

www.latimes.com (March 2007)

www.obama.senate.gov

www.wikipedia.org

Websites for Punahou School, Occidental College, Columbia University, Harvard University, Hawaii, Kenya, Indonesia.

Magazines and Newspapers

Boston Globe: January 2007

Fortune, July 2007

International Herald Tribune, April 27, 2007.

Newsweek, September 2006, December 2006, January 2007, May 2007, June 2007, July 2007

The New York Times: February 1990; July 2007;

Time: October 2006, July 2007

Travel Smart: September 2005.

Numerous television programs and a rally on the Boston Common where Senator Obama appeared with Governor Deval Patrick.

Acknowledgments

With special thanks to Cindy Davidsmeyer, Tom Wilson, George Moffett, Debra Lawless, Evelyn Reading, Michael Mallon, Rod Nordell, Laurence Tribe, Senator Edward M. Kennedy, and a host of others.

978-0-595-51404-5
0-595-51404-9

Printed in the United States
203384BV00003B/1-105/P

9 780595 514045